My First Book of
JAPANESE
WORDS

Dedicated to Mariko, Eri, Yuri, and the late
Munetsugu Yamazaki, my Japanese family. Thank
you for opening your hearts and home to me—
then and now. You have enriched my life.—MHB

My First Book of
JAPANESE
WORDS

An ABC Rhyming Book

By Michelle Haney Brown

illustrated by Aya Padrón

TUTTLE Publishing

Tokyo | Rutland, Vermont | Singapore

Published by Tuttle Publishing, an imprint of Periplus Editions (HK) Ltd.

www.tuttlepublishing.com

Library of Congress Cataloging-in-Publication Data for this title is in progress.

ISBN 978-4-8053-1201-8

Distributed by

North America, Latin America & Europe
Tuttle Publishing, 364 Innovation Drive
North Clarendon, VT 05759-9436 U.S.A.
Tel: 1 (802) 773-8930; Fax: 1 (802) 773-6993
info@tuttlepublishing.com; www.tuttlepublishing.com

Japan
Tuttle Publishing, Yaekari Building,
3rd Floor, 5-4-12 Osaki, Shinagawa-ku
Tokyo 141 0032
Tel: (81) 3 5437-0171; Fax: (81) 3 5437-0755
sales@tuttle.co.jp; www.tuttle.co.jp

Asia Pacific
Berkeley Books Pte. Ltd.
61 Tai Seng Avenue #02-12
Singapore 534167
Tel: (65) 6280-1330; Fax: (65) 6280-6290
inquiries@periplus.com.sg; www.periplus.com

Indonesia
PT Java Books Indonesia
Kawasan Industri Pulogadung
Jl. Rawa Gelam IV No. 9
Jakarta 13930
Tel: (62) 21 4682-1088; Fax: (62) 21 461-0206
cs@javabooks.co.id; www.periplus.com

First edition

19 18 17 16
10 9 8 7 6 5 4 3 2

Printed in Hong Kong   1604EP

ABOUT TUTTLE
"Books to Span the East and West"

Our core mission at Tuttle Publishing is to create books which bring people together one page at a time. Tuttle was founded in 1832 in the small New England town of Rutland, Vermont (USA). Our fundamental values remain as strong today as they were then—to publish best-in-class books informing the English-speaking world about the countries and peoples of Asia. The world has become a smaller place today and Asia's economic, cultural and political influence has expanded, yet the need for meaningful dialogue and information about this diverse region has never been greater. Since 1948, Tuttle has been a leader in publishing books on the cultures, arts, cuisines, languages and literatures of Asia. Our authors and photographers have won numerous awards and Tuttle has published thousands of books on subjects ranging from martial arts to paper crafts. We welcome you to explore the wealth of information available on Asia at **www.tuttlepublishing.com**.

Author's Preface

The goal of *My First Book of Japanese Words* is to introduce young children to Japanese language and culture through simple everyday words; many of them are shared by children everywhere, while others are specific to Japanese culture. The words in this book are presented in Kanji (when applicable), Kana, and Romanized form (Romaji).

Kanji is the pictographic system of characters originally borrowed from Chinese. In general, each character represents a word, but can sometimes be combined with others to form compound words or express different meanings.

If a word is written in characters, it can always be written phonetically as well. There are two phonetic alphabets in Japanese. *Hiragana* is used for Japanese words and is the first system of writing that children learn. *Katakana* is most often used for words that have been borrowed from other languages or for words that represent sounds. These two writing systems are referred to jointly as *kana*.

Certain English consonants are not present in Japanese. In this book the letters L, Q, V and W are represented by the Japanese equivalents of the words *lion*, *queen*, *vegetables* and *xylophone*. Raion (lion) shows how a word can be shared between very different languages. And because the interpretation of sounds is a part of any language, the word *nyah* (meow) appears in one of the rhymes to help show that different languages have their own words to mimic the sounds we hear.

A note on pronunciation:

A is pronounced "ah" as in "father."

E is pronounced as in "let."

I is pronounced "ee" as in "meet."

O is pronounced as in "go," but softer, with an open mouth.

Ō is also a long o sound, but is held longer, for two beats

U is pronounced "oo" as in "moon," but softer, with a more open mouth

G is pronounced as in "goat" rather than as in "gem."

R is generally a flap of the tongue from the roof of the mouth to the bottom, behind the teeth—sort of a combination of "l" and "d."

F is a soft sound, closer to an "h," accompanied with a blow. Teeth don't touch lip.

To listen to the Japanese words in this book visit the book's page on www.tuttlepublishing.com.

My hope is that this book will spark in your kids not only an interest in Japanese, but also a desire for intercultural understanding, a feeling of curiosity about the world, and a sense that while there are differences between peoples, we all have much in common.

Have fun reading!

あり
蟻

A is for *ari*.
A teeny weeny
ant crawls
with teeny
weeny legs on
the bamboo plant.

ぶた
豚

B is for *buta*,
A piggy so cute!
She likes to dance
and play her flute.

ちょうちょう
蝶々

C is for *chōchō*,
a butterfly bright —
red and purple, blue
and white.

でんしゃ
電車 D is for *dēnsha* — a train in Japan — goes choo choo down the track as fast as it can.

F is for *futon*, a Japanese bed —
spread out on tatami, make dreams in your head.

ふとん
布団

A futon is an old-fashioned Japanese bed. It is like a thick, soft quilt, with a fluffy quilt to cover up with. The futon is usually placed on a straw mat floor. In Japan a lot of people use beds now, but some people still use futons.

がっこう
学校

G is for *gakkō*,
the word for school,
where we make
lots of friends and
learning is cool.

Chopsticks look tricky but they are fun to use once you get used to them. In Japan, rice grains are short and stick together when they are cooked, so it's easy to pick up a clump of rice with your chopsticks.

はし
箸

H is for *hashi*. Chopsticks are nice for picking up goodies like veggies and rice.

いぬ
犬

I is for *inu* —
dogs that bark.
My dog and I like
to walk in the park.

ジャンケン/
じゃんけん
janken

J is for *Janken*,
a game played in
Japan. It's Rock,
Paper, Scissors
(make those with
your hand).

In Japan, people take off their outdoor shoes before they go into a house or school and leave them in a special place until they are ready to go back outside.

くつ

靴

K is for *kutsu*, the outdoor shoes. So many pairs here! Which ones are whose?

ライオン
獅子

L is a letter not used everywhere. Lion is *raion* and gives you a scare.

The Japanese language doesn't have an L, Q, V, or X sound, but Japanese does use some words that come from other languages. *Raion* comes from the English word Lion.

みみ
耳

M is for *mimi*.
This word means ear —
a left one, a right one
We use them to hear.

ねこ
猫

N is for *neko*,
a kitty so sweet.
She says "nyah"
when she wants
a treat.

Even animal sounds
have different
words in different
languages. In English,
the word for a cat
sound is "meow" but
in Japan a cat says
"nyah" instead.

おにぎり
お握り

O is *onigiri*,
a Japanese
treat —
a rice ball
that's yummy
and fun to eat!

Onigiri are easy to carry
and to eat at a picnic, or
while you're riding on a
bullet train.

パン

Some Japanese bread looks just like the kind of bread we see every day, but sometimes the bread is shaped into rolls and stuffed with tasty fillings. "Oishii!" is a word for "Yummy!"

P is for *pan* —
bread, soft and white,
filled with sweet bean
paste. Oishii! Take a bite!

じょおう
女王

Q is for queen —
a *joō* wears a crown,
a bright-colored sash
and a beautiful gown.

Remember, Q
is one of the
sounds you
won't find in
the Japanese
language.

れい
礼

R is for *rei*.
We bow when we say
"Good morning" and
"Thank you" and
"Have a good day."

In Japan everyone bows when they
say things like "Hello," "Good-bye,"
"Thank you" and "I'm sorry."

せんせい
先生

S is for *sensei.*
My teacher is good
and helps me learn
all the things that
I should.

たぬき
狸

T is for *tanuki.*
This furry guy is a
raccoon dog with
a twinkly eye.

Some animals live in some countries
but not in others. Raccoon dogs
don't live in the United States and
skunks don't live in Japan.

うま
馬

U is for *uma*,
a beautiful horse.
He likes to eat
hay and carrots,
of course.

V is for the veggies we eat all day long. We call them yasai here. They help us grow strong.

やさい
野菜

Remember, there's no V sound in Japanese, but there are plenty of veggies. In Japan, you might even have yasai at breakfast!

W is for *Waa!*
which is how we
say "Wow!" (Maybe
you'll say it now
that you know how.)

ワー／
わあ

もっきん
木琴

X is for Xylophone —
give it a pound! We call it a
mokkin. It has a great sound!

Japanese doesn't have
an X sound, but Japan
definitely has xylophones.
In Japan, the mokkin is
usually made of wood.

ヤッタ！
やった！

Y is for *yatta*
"I did it!" "Yay!"
This is a word
I like to say.

For a long time a lot of people have believed that elephants are afraid of mice, and hop and dance and run away when they see them. What do you believe?

象

Z is for *zō*, an elephant BIG — but if he sees a mouse, he might dance a jig.